Oxford University Press

Oxford University Press, Great Clarendon Street, Oxford OX2 6DP

Oxford   New York
Athens   Auckland   Bangkok   Bogota   Bombay
Buenos Aires   Calcutta   Cape Town   Dar es Salaam   Delhi
Florence   Hong Kong   Istanbul   Karachi
Kuala Lumpur   Madras   Madrid   Melbourne
Mexico City   Nairobi   Paris   Singapore
Taipei   Tokyo   Toronto

and associated companies in
Berlin   Ibadan

OXFORD and OXFORD ENGLISH
are trade marks of Oxford University Press

ISBN International edition 0 19 435120 3
ISBN Egyptian edition 0 19 435092 4

© Oxford University Press 1997

No unauthorized photocopying

Illustrations by David Mostyn, Lynne Willey, David Lock, Oxford Illustrators,
Pythia Ashton-Jewell, Ian Heard, Pete Lawrence, Tony Morris, Frank Hill

Photographs by Greg Evans International (pp. 30, 31, 38, 56, 59, 60), Rex Features Ltd (pp. 60, 77),
International Education Unit, Oxford University Press (pp. 30, 31, 60, 64)

Designed and typeset by Oxprint Design, Oxford

Printed in Hong Kong

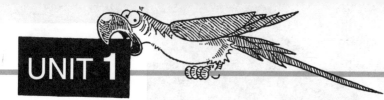

UNIT 1

❶ Write

My name's Tom.

My name's Susan.

I like playing football.

I've got a cat.

I've been to a wildlife park.

I went to London last year.

I'll get up late on Saturday.

I'm going to my gran's tomorrow.

I was washing my hair.

I've had my bike for two years.

1 He says his name's Tom. _____

2 She says her _____

3 _____

4 _____

5 _____

6 _____

7 _____

8 _____

9 _____

10 _____

❷ Write about yesterday and tomorrow

Every day I go home after school and have a drink. After that I do my homework. Then I watch TV with my sister for an hour. At six o'clock we have dinner with Mum and Dad. After dinner I play with my friends. At nine o'clock I go to bed and read for half an hour. Then I fall asleep.

Yesterday Tom went home after school _____

_____

_____

_____

Tomorrow he'll go home after school _____

_____

_____

_____

3 Complete the answers

1 Are you learning English?   Yes, <u>I am.</u>

2 Have you got a pen?   Yes, _____

3 Do you like watching TV?   Yes, _____

4 Can you write your name?   Yes, _____

5 Have you ever eaten rice?   Yes, _____

6 Were you tired last night?   Yes, _____

7 Will you go to bed tonight?   Yes, _____

8 Did you brush your teeth
   yesterday?   Yes, _____

4 Write the words in order

your   *address?*   *What's*

1 your   address   what's   <u>What's your address?</u>

2 who   with   do   live   you   _____?

3 do   weekend   what   at   the   you   did   _____?

4 what   do   will   tomorrow   you   _____?

5 which   you   go   school   do   to   _____?

6 how   had   long   this   you   book   have   _____?

7 free   what   time   your   do   do   in   you   _____?

8 what   7 o'clock   this   were   morning   _____

   you   doing   at   _____?

5 Write your answers for exercise 4

1 My address is _____

2 _____

3 _____

4 _____

5 _____

6 _____

7 _____

8 _____

UNIT 2

❶ Read and write

Remember!

I'd like to swim.	Would you like to swim?	Yes, I would.
I wouldn't like to fly.	Would you like to fly?	No, I wouldn't.
He'd like to swim.	Would ____ like to swim?	Yes, ____ would.
____ wouldn't like to fly.	Would _____ to fly?	No, _____ .
She'd _____ to swim.	_____ to swim?	Yes, _____ .
_____ to fly.	_____ to fly?	No, _____ .

❷ Write

cold   famous   funny   interesting   new   sunny

1   He'd like to drink <u>something cold.</u>

2   She'd like to read _____

3   He'd like _____

_____

4   She'd _____

5   _____

_____

6   _____

_____

③ Find the words

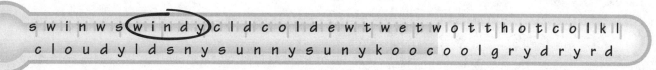

s w i n w s w i n d y c l d c o l d e w t w e t w o t t h o t c o l k l
c l o u d y l d s n y s u n n y s u n y k o o c o o l g r y d r y r d

④ Write

1   In Bath today the weather is _windy_ and _____

_____

2   In Brighton it's _____

_____

3   In London _____

⑤ Write about your weather today

_____

_____

6 **Write questions for your friend**

QUESTIONS

1 Would you like to _____ ?

2 Would you like _____ ?

3 Would you _____ ?

4 Would _____ ?

5 _____ ?

6 _____ ?

7 **Answer your friend's questions**

ANSWERS

1 _____

2 _____

3 _____

4 _____

5 _____

6 _____

8 **Write about your friend**

1 My friend _____

2 _____

3 _____

4 _____

5 _____

6 _____

UNIT 3

❶ Write

DOWN ↓

1

2

4

7

8

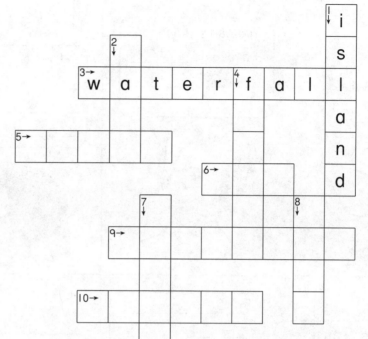

ACROSS → 3  5  6

9  10

❷ Write

 1 They're <u>flying</u>
                          <u>over a river.</u>

 4 _____
                          _____

2 They're <u>turning</u>
   _____

 5 _____
                          _____

3 They're _____
   _____

6 _____
   _____

❸ Write

1

I'd like to go to Wet 'n' Wild. What can you do there?

You can swim in real waves and _____ _____ _____

2

I'd like to go to _____ _____ _____ ?

You can watch birds, fish and alligators.

3

I'd like to go to Seaworld. What _____ _____ ?

_____ _____ _____ _____

4

_____ _____ _____ ?

You can visit the Space Shuttle Launch Site.

❹ Odd one out

1 alligator   dolphin   people   turtle   _____

2 north   right   south   west   _____

3 blue   green   real   yellow   _____

4 autumn   summer   today   winter   _____

5 city   house   town   village   _____

6 lake   mountain   river   sea   _____

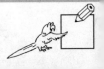

5 Write

1   If you look down now, you can <u>see a</u>
    <u>waterfall</u>.

2   If you look down now, you can _____
    _____

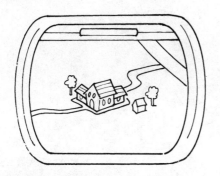

3   If you look down now, _____
    _____

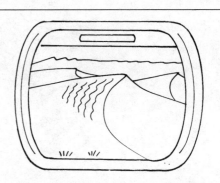

4   If you _____
    _____

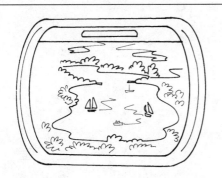

5   _____
    _____

6   _____
    _____

6 Write about places you know

1   If you go to _____ , you can _____

2   If you go to _____ , you _____

3   If you _____

4   _____

UNIT 4

1 Write about you

1 Would you like to go to America? _____

2 Would you like to go to Florida? _____

3 Would you like to go to Disney World? _____

4 Would you like to go to Wet 'n' Wild? _____

2 Find the words and write

a	r	r	i	v	e	d	i
c	t	r	u	i	h	s	e
p	o	w	a	s	a	w	n
h	o	e	f	i	d	a	j
v	k	r	y	t	i	m	o
l	s	e	w	e	n	t	y
l	i	k	e	d	t	u	e
p	g	s	h	o	w	e	d

are	were
arrive	
enjoy	
go	
have	
is	

like
see
show
swim
take
visit

❸ Write

6 January

Today we <u>went</u> to the Everglades in the south of Florida.

We _____ the National Park. We _____ a trip on

a special boat with a park ranger. It _____ very interesting.

The park ranger _____ us lots of birds and animals. We _____ alligators,

turtles and flamingos. I _____ the alligators best. They've got enormous teeth.

We _____ very lucky – we _____ a manatee too. I _____ lots of photos.

Susan

❹ Write

alligator   deer   dolphin   flamingo   manatee   turtle

1   flamingo

2   _____

3   _____

4   _____

5   _____

6   _____

❺ Write your diary for yesterday

_____

_____

_____

_____

_____

6 Write

1 Tom and Susan <u>went</u> to Florida.

2 They _____ the Everglades National Park.

3 They _____ a boat trip with a park ranger.

4 They _____ a manatee in the water.

5 They _____ to Wet 'n' Wild.

6 They _____ in waves just like the sea.

7 Write

blue   dolphin   dry   hot   manatee   north   red   south
spring   summer   sunny   turtle   west   white   winter

alligator	<u>dolphin</u>	_____	_____
autumn	_____	_____	_____
black	_____	_____	_____
cool	_____	_____	_____
east	_____	_____	_____

8 Write

It's _____   It's _____   _____   _____

⑨ Match

1 I'd like to go ——————————— someone interesting.

2 Would you like to go ————— somewhere interesting.

3 I'd like to meet something interesting.

4 Would you like to meet something different?

5 I'd like to do somewhere different?

6 Would you like to read someone different?

⑩ Complete the answers

1 Would Tom like to see Mickey Mouse? Yes, <u>he would.</u>

2 Would Susan like to stay at home? No, _____

3 Would you like to go to Disney World? Yes, _____

4 Would you like to swim with an alligator? No, _____

5 Can you watch animals at Seaworld? Yes, _____

6 Can you go swimming at Seaworld? No, _____

⑪ Write

1 idliketogotoamerica <u>I'd like to go to America.</u>

2 dolphinscantfly _____

3 theyreflyingovernewyork _____

4 ifyoulookdownyoucanseethesea

_____

5 whensusanwasinfloridashekeptadiary

_____

6 manateesareslowanimals

_____

12

UNIT 5

❶ Write

1 Susan can swim <u>faster</u> than Tom.

2 Ben is two years _____ than Tom.

3 Ben swam more _____ than Susan.

4 Ben swam the _____

❷ Write the words in order

1 race let's have a

<u>Let's have a race.</u>

2 faster can't me than you swim

_____

3 can you I easily beat

_____

4 well swim he can really

_____

5 quickly brother she swam more her than

_____

13

❸ Write

badly	worse	the worst
well	_____	the best
quietly	more quietly	_____
slowly	_____	the slowest
easily	_____	the most easily
loudly	more loudly	_____

Remember!

❹ Match

1

Touch your toes.　　Turn your head.

4

2

Swing your arms.　　Clap your hands.

5

3

Bend your knees.　　Stamp your feet.

6

❺ Write about you

Bend your knees slowly.

Stand up quickly.

Clap your hands quietly.

Stamp your feet loudly.

1 I can bend my knees slowly.

2 _____

3 _____

4 _____

UNIT 5

6 Odd one out

1 beat   bend   race   swim   _____

2 easily   fastest   quickly   quietly   _____

3 class   head   knees   toes   _____

4 swing   touch   turn   walk   _____

5 better   faster   more slowly   well   _____

7 Write

Swing your _____ .

One, two, three.

_____ them more slowly.

Do it like me.

Don't _____ them so _____ .

It's easy, you see.

8 Choose and write

_____ your _____ .

One, two, three.

_____ _____ _____ _____ .

Do it like me.

Don't _____ _____ so _____ .

It's easy, you see.

1 Write

?

```
            MENU
b u r g e r

c _ _ _

l _ _ _ _ _ _

i _ _ _ _ _ _

s _ _ _ _ _ _

c _ _ _ _ _
```

2 Match and write

If you eat too many chips,	you'll be sick.
If you play too much tennis,	you'll be hungry.
If you drink too much cola,	you'll get fat.
If you don't eat something,	you'll be thirsty.
If you don't drink something,	you'll get hot.

1   If you eat too many chips, you'll get fat.

2   _____

3   _____

4   _____

5   _____

3 **Write**   cold   hot   late   old   tired   wet

1   It's too <u>hot</u> to play tennis.

2   If it rains, we'll get _____

3   If you don't wear a sweater, you'll be _____

4   Tom was too _____ to do his homework.

5   My dad's too _____ to play football.

6   Yesterday she was _____ for her English class.

4 **Write**

good for you	bad for you
apples	chips
_____	_____
_____	_____
_____	_____

chips

_____

apples

_____

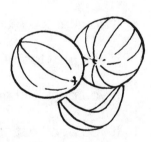

_____

_____

_____

_____

UNIT 6

⑤ Write

1 You <u>shouldn't</u> drink too much cola.

2 Ice cream is very _____

3 Burgers and chips have got a lot of _____ in them.

4 Bread and rice are both _____ for you.

5 If you're hungry, eat an _____

6 Fruit and vegetables are _____ good for you.

⑥ Write questions for your friend

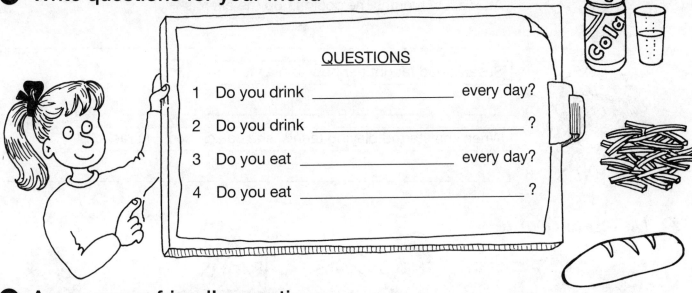

QUESTIONS

1 Do you drink _____ every day?

2 Do you drink _____ ?

3 Do you eat _____ every day?

4 Do you eat _____ ?

⑦ Answer your friend's questions

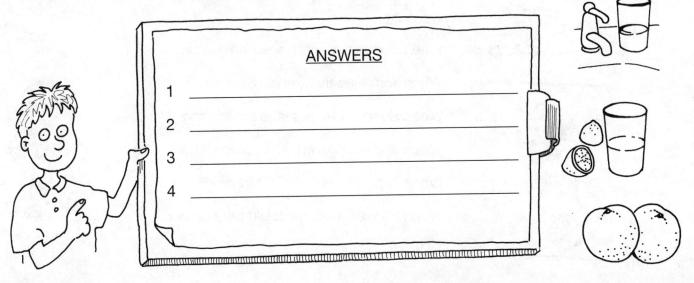

ANSWERS

1 _____

2 _____

3 _____

4 _____

UNIT 7

❶ Correct the sentences

| When Richard was young, he couldn't run. |

1 When Richard was young, he could run for miles.

| Richard can't walk now. |

2 _____

| Tom was very fit last year. |

3 _____

| After a few months, he couldn't do the exercises. |

4 _____

| Susan's dad taught her how to play tennis. |

5 _____

| When she started playing tennis, she could use a big racket. |

6 _____

❷ Match and write

When Susan was one, she could walk. | f |

When Tom was five, he could write. | |

When Susan was four, she could read. | |

When she was seven, she could dance. | |

When Tom was two, he could paint. | |

When he was nine, he could play tennis. | |

3 Write questions for your friend

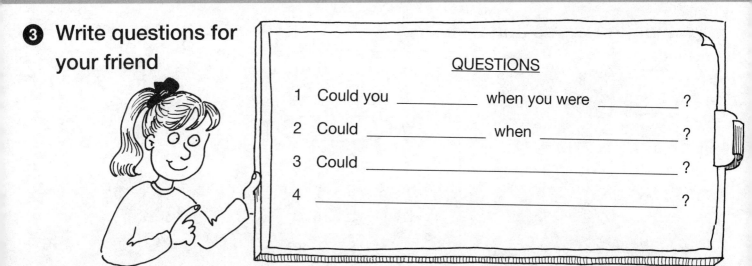

QUESTIONS

1 Could you _____ when you were _____ ?

2 Could _____ when _____ ?

3 Could _____ ?

4 _____ ?

4 Answer your friend's questions

ANSWERS

1 _____

2 _____

3 _____

4 _____

5 Write about your friend

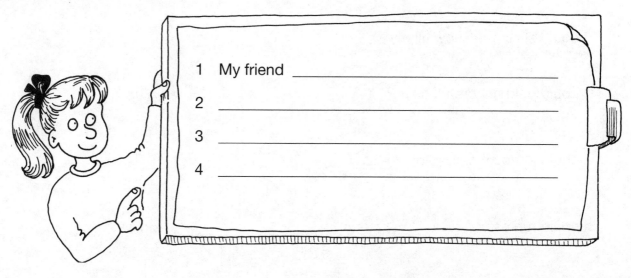

1 My friend _____

2 _____

3 _____

4 _____

6 ## Find the words and write

1 club

r	a	v	t	u	p
a	l	m	i	t	e
c	w	c	l	u	b
k	a	r	a	t	e
e	l	o	y	e	l
t	k	r	u	n	t
o	r	y	c	n	m
p	o	s	t	i	m
l	n	t	o	s	g

2 _____

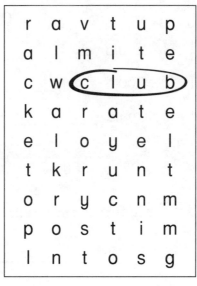

6 _____

5 _____

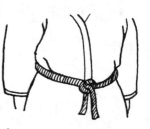

3 _____

4 _____

7 ## Write

When I was young, I could touch my toes.

I could catch a ball on the end of my _____

I could ski in the snow till my _____ froze.

I could hold my breath till my  _____ turned blue.

I could jump as high as a  _____

I could run as fast as a _____ too.

UNIT 8

1 Rewrite the sentences

1 My friend can write more carefully than anyone in our class.

<u>My friend is the most careful</u> writer in our class.

2 My sister can sing more quietly than anyone in our family.

_____ singer in our family.

3 My cousin can swim faster than anyone in the club.

_____ swimmer in the club.

4 My friend can run more quickly than anyone in our school.

_____ runner in our school.

2 Write about your friends and family

1 My friend _____

2 _____

3 _____

4 _____

3 Complete the answers

1 Can Tom sing more loudly than Ben?   Yes, <u>he can.</u>

2 Can Susan walk the quickest?   No, _____

3 Can Ben speak more quietly than Tom?   Yes, _____

4 Can Tom write more carefully than Ben?   No, _____

5 Can Susan read better than Tom?   Yes, _____

6 Can Tom swim the fastest?   No, _____

4 Choose and write

1 You should eat a lot of fruit.   [should / shouldn't]

2 Oranges _____ good for you.   [are / aren't]

3 If you brush your teeth, _____ get toothache.   [you'll / you won't]

4 If you want to be healthy, you _____ drink a lot of water. [must / mustn't]

5 Choose and write

I know melon is [are / is] good for you, but I don't like _____

[it / them]. I don't like fruit. I like chocolate. I like biscuits too. I know they

_____ [aren't / isn't] very good for you but I like _____

[it / them]. Chocolate biscuits _____ [are / is] my favourites!

6 Write

I know beans _____ good for you, but I don't like

_____ . I don't like vegetables. I like cakes. I like ice cream

too. I know it _____ very good for you but I like

_____ . Coffee ice cream _____ my favourite!

7 Write about you

I know _____

_____

_____

8 Write

I'm too old to run now.

1   Richard is too old to run now.

I take my dog for a walk every day.

2 _____

At first I didn't like the karate club.

3 _____

Last month I won my red belt.

4 _____

I started playing tennis three years ago.

5 _____

After a year, I could use a big racket.

6 _____

9 Write could or couldn't

1   When my mother was three, she _____ speak English.

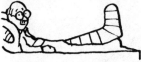

2   When Richard broke his leg, he _____ walk.

3   When Susan was nine, she _____ ride a bike.

4   When my father was young, he _____ swim very well.

10 Write

1 I like <u>eating</u> cakes.

2 Susan's favourite sport is _____

3 When I was young, I could touch my _____

4 I can swim, but I can't _____

5 If you eat a lot of _____ , you'll be healthy.

6 I think _____ is a difficult sport.

e	a	t	i	n	g
	e				
		e			
			e		
				e	
					e

11 Write your own words and sentences

1 _____

2 _____

3 _____

4 _____

5 _____

6 _____

e					
	e				
		e			
			e		
				e	
					e

12 Odd one out

1 hand   head   knee   orange   _____

2 better   faster   loudly   worse   _____

3 burgers   chips   chocolate   cola   _____

4 bored   more   sick   wet   _____

5 bend   jump   read   turn   _____

UNIT 9

1 Write

1 I like geography.   So do I.   I don't.

2 I went to a theme park last year.   So _____   I _____

3 I've been to America.   So _____   I _____

4 I'm going on holiday in the summer.   So _____   I _____

5 I'd like to go to Paris.   So _____   I _____

6 I've got a map of the world.   So _____   I _____

2 Write sentences about you

1 I'm _____   So am I.

2 _____   I haven't.

3 _____   So would I.

4 _____   I didn't.

5 _____   So have I.

6 _____   I don't.

3 Write sentences for your friend

1 I _____

2 I _____

3 I _____

4 I _____

4 Reply to your friend's sentences

REPLIES

1 _____

2 _____

3 _____

4 _____

⑤ Write numbers

a   forty   <u>40</u>

b   one hundred and eighty   _____

c   three hundred   _____

d   one thousand, five hundred   _____

e   two thousand   _____

f   three thousand, five hundred   _____

⑥ Match

1   The Great Barrier Reef   is in China.

                                        is in France.

2   The Taj Mahal   is in India.

                                        is in Australia.

3   The Great Wall   is more than 2000 years old.

                                        is more than 300 metres high.

4   The Eiffel Tower   is more than 1500 kilometres long.

                                        is more than 300 years old.

⑦ Write about a famous place in your country

_____

_____

_____

_____

❽ Read and write

1   It isn't made of stone and earth.   It isn't the Great Wall of China.

   It isn't made of coral.   It isn't _____

   It isn't made of iron.   It isn't _____

                                         It's _____

2   It isn't made of iron.   It isn't _____

   It isn't made of stone and earth.   It isn't _____

   It isn't made of marble.   It isn't _____

                                         It's _____

❾ Write

 1   This head is made of marble.

 2   This necklace _____

3   This _____

 4   _____

 5   _____

 6   _____

UNIT 10

① Read and write

That bird is so small.	That is such a small bird.
Those birds are so small.	Those are such small birds.

That animal is _____ big.   That is _____ big animal.

Those animals are _____ .   Those are _____ .

② Write

1 The kangaroo has got <u>such a</u> strong tail. It can kill a man.

4 Koala bears are _____ good climbers. They can climb easily and quickly. They climb to the top of trees and eat the new leaves.

2 Emus are _____ tall birds. They are sometimes two metres tall.

5 Kangaroos are _____ fast. They can run at 65 kilometres per hour.

3 The kookaburra is _____ strong bird. It can kill a snake.

6 The emu is _____ fast. It runs very quickly but it can't fly.

❸ Write numbers

a nine   9

b forty-seven   _____

c three hundred and fifty   _____

d six thousand, three hundred   _____

e forty thousand   _____

f three hundred thousand   _____

g one million, two hundred thousand   _____

h seventeen and a half million   _____

❹ Write

1 Is Australia a continent?   Yes, it is.

2 Did the first people land in Australia in 1770?   _____

3 Is Sydney the capital of Australia?   _____

4 Has Australia got a population of more than ten million? _____

5 Were most Australians born in Australia?   _____

6 Do most people live in the interior?   _____

7 Did Ernest Giles see Ayers Rock in 1770?   _____

8 Can kangaroos jump very high?   _____

5 Read and write

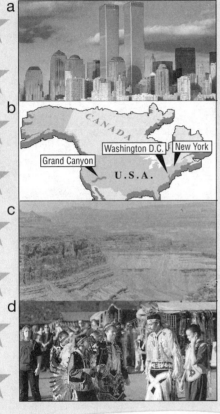

a

b

c

d

⭐ 1 The United States of America is the world's fourth largest country in area and the third largest in population. More than 255 million people live there.

⭐ 2 The biggest and most famous city is New York. It has a population of more than seven million. The capital city, with a population of nearly four million, is Washington D.C.

⭐ 3 When the first Europeans arrived in North America in the early 17th century, many native Americans (or American Indians) were already living there. The first people arrived in North America 40,000 years ago from Asia.

⭐ 4 The Grand Canyon is a huge canyon on the Colorado river in the interior of the United States. It is 350 kilometres long, between six and twenty-nine kilometres wide and nearly 1.5 kilometres deep.

1 When did the first people arrive in North America?

<u>40,000 years ago.</u>

2 Who arrived in North America in the early 17th century?

_____

3 What is the capital of the United States?

_____

4 How many people live in the capital?

_____

5 Where is the Grand Canyon?

_____

6 How deep is it?

_____

UNIT 11

1 Find the countries and write

1 A <u>m e r i c a</u>

2 A _ _ _ _ _ _ _ _ _

3 B _ _ _ _ _ _ _

4 C _ _ _ _ _

5 E _ _ _ _ _

6 F _ _ _ _ _ _

7 G _ _ _ _ _ _

8 I _ _ _ _ _

9 M _ _ _ _ _ _

10 V _ _ _ _ _ _ _ _ _

A	U	S	T	R	A	L	I	A
P	Z	V	J	U	M	L	M	N
H	L	G	R	E	E	C	E	M
C	V	R	S	T	R	I	G	E
B	R	I	T	A	I	N	Y	X
A	N	T	V	U	C	D	P	I
X	C	H	I	N	A	I	T	C
F	R	A	N	C	E	A	X	O
V	E	N	E	Z	U	E	L	A

2 Write

apples   corn   cotton   grapes   potatoes   rice   tomatoes   wheat

 1 <u>Grapes are grown here.</u>

 2 _____ is grown here.

 3 _____ grown here.

 4 _____ here.

 5 _____

 6 _____

 7 _____

 8 _____

3 **True (✔) or false (✗)?**

1 Tea is grown in India. ✓

2 Coffee is grown in America. ☐

3 Radios are made in China. ☐

4 Planes are built in America. ☐

4 **Write**

1 Tea isn't grown in America.

2 Coffee _____ grown in India.

3 Radios _____ made in America.

4 Planes _____ built in India.

5 **Write**

1 They don't build ✈ in Venezuela.

Planes aren't built in Venezuela.

2 They make 📻 in Britain.

_____

3 They grow 🍚 in Mexico.

_____

4 They don't grow ☕ in France.

_____

5 They make 🚗 in Italy.

_____

6 They grow 🍇 in Greece.

_____

6 Write about your country

1 Is cotton grown? _____

2 Are radios made? _____

3 Is oil produced? _____

4 Are grapes grown? _____

5 Is coal produced? _____

7 Complete the sentences about your country

1 Potatoes _____

2 Wheat _____

3 Cars _____

4 Planes _____

5 Gas _____

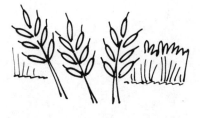

8 Write five other sentences about your country

1 _____

2 _____

3 _____

4 _____

5 _____

1 Write *asked* or *said*

1 One day Chen's master <u>said</u>, 'Go to the forest and chop some wood.'

2 'What's the matter, Chen?' the old man _____ .

3 'My axe has fallen into the river,' Chen _____ . 'I can't chop any wood and my master will be angry with me.'

4 'Don't cry,' the old man _____ . 'I'll get it for you.'

5 'Is this your axe?' he _____ .

6 'Yes,' Chen _____ . 'That's my axe.'

7 'You're an honest boy, Chen,' the old man _____ . 'This axe will work hard for you.'

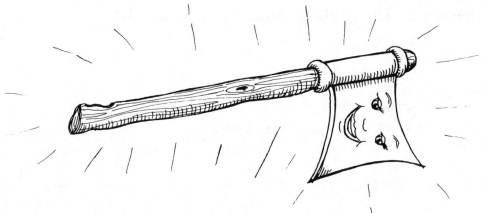

2 Write

1 sit down chen the axe said I'll chop the wood for you

'Sit down, Chen,' the axe said. _____

2 thank you magic axe said chen

_____

3 well done chen his master said you have cut a lot of wood today

_____

4 i did not cut this wood chen said

_____

5 you are a stupid boy his master said why didn't you take the axe made of gold

_____

❸ Write

DOWN ↓

1 Chen walked across a <u>bridge</u>.

2 Chen's axe wasn't made

of _____

4 'You're an _____ boy,
Chen,' the old man said.

6 The old man _____
up an axe.

7 Chen put all the wood into

his _____

9 Chen's axe fell into the _____

13 The old man had a

_____ white beard.

14 'What's the _____ ,
Chen?' the old man asked.

18 Chen's master was _____ when he
heard about the gold and silver axes.

19 'Don't _____ ,' said the old man. 'I'll
get your axe for you.'

21 Chen told his master about the old man
_____ the beard.

22 Chen said, 'I can't chop any _____ .'

24 Suddenly Chen saw an _____ man.

ACROSS →

3 Chen's master said, 'Go to the forest and
<u>chop</u> some wood.'

5 Chen worked for a _____ man.

8 Chen's axe was made of _____

10 'I _____ not cut this wood,' Chen
told his master.

11 Chen's master was very _____ when
he saw the wood in Chen's basket.

12 Chen's axe wasn't made of _____

15 Chen's master began to _____ Chen.

16 Chen's _____ was a rich man.

17 Chen said, 'This is a _____ axe.'

20 The magic axe _____ the wood in
Chen's basket.

23 Chen went to the _____ to chop
some wood.

25 Chen was a _____ boy.

26 '_____ are a stupid boy,' Chen's
master said.

27 Chen's master said, 'You have cut a lot of

wood _____ .'

36

❹ Write replies

1	I like kangaroos.	So do I.
2	I've swum in the sea.	I _____
3	I've got a test tomorrow.	So _____
4	I live in a village.	I _____
5	I liked the story about Chen.	So _____
6	I'm going to read another story.	I _____
7	I'd like to go to China.	So _____
8	I had a test last week.	I _____

❺ Write sentences about Australia

1 Wheat is grown.

2 Planes _____

3 Coal _____

4 Grapes _____

5 Radios _____

6 Gold _____

7 Cars _____

8 Coffee _____

6 Write in or of

1 The Great Barrier Reef is made of coral.

2 The Taj Mahal is ___ India.

3 Chen's axe was made ___ iron.

4 Cars are made ___ China.

5 The Eiffel Tower is ___ the centre ___ Paris.

6 Canberra is the capital ___ Australia.

7 Most Australians live ___ cities.

8 They eat rice ___ the south ___ China.

9 They make lots ___ things in China.

10 The highest waterfall ___ the world is ___ Venezuela.

7 Write so or such

1 The Taj Mahal is such a beautiful building.

2 Chen was _____ an honest boy.

3 Ayers Rock is _____ big – it is nine kilometres round.

4 Chen's master was _____ angry – he began to beat Chen.

5 There's _____ much to see and do in America.

6 Tom and Susan had _____ a wonderful time in Australia.

8 Write

> asked   began   came   dropped   fell   held   jumped
> looked   said   saw   spoke   took   was   went

One day Chen took his axe and _____ to the forest to chop some wood.

He _____ to a bridge across the river. He _____ his axe and

it _____ into the water. Chen _____ to cry. Suddenly he _____

an old man. The old man _____ to Chen. Then he _____ into the

water. The old man _____ up an axe. 'Is this your axe?' he _____ .

Chen _____ at the axe. It _____ made of silver. 'No,' he _____ .
'That's not my axe.'

UNIT 13

1 Write   already   ever   just   never   yet

1 Tom hasn't read 'Pop Stars' <u>yet</u>.

2 Has Susan _____ been to a pop concert?

3 No, she's _____ been to a pop concert.

4 She's _____ bought his latest CD.

5 She's _____ got a poster of Ziggy in her room.

2 Find the words and write

a	b	i	t	s	y	u	w	p	t
c	v	b	n	i	m	w	e	o	h
r	t	c	y	n	u	i	o	s	p
c	a	o	s	g	d	f	t	t	g
w	i	n	t	e	r	v	i	e	w
d	f	c	g	r	h	i	c	r	o
e	r	e	t	y	u	d	k	i	p
p	o	r	u	v	i	d	e	o	t
c	v	t	i	t	g	h	t	j	e

1   interview

2   _____

3   _____

4   _____

5   _____

6   _____

③ Write the words in order

1 yet haven't tickets I got

   I haven't got tickets yet.

   I haven't got tickets yet

2 I've latest his seen just video

   _____

3 concerts pop been two already he's to

   _____

4 London been never she's to

   _____

5 Ziggy met you ever have

   _____ ?

④ Choose and write

1 Ziggy's plane has landed.

   [is landing / has landed]

2 The door of the plane _____

   [is opening / has opened]

3 Ziggy _____ out of the plane.

   [is stepping / has stepped]

4 A girl _____ flowers at Ziggy.

   [is throwing / has thrown]

5 An interviewer _____ to Ziggy.

   [is speaking / has spoken]

6 Ziggy _____ into a car.

   [is getting / has got]

5 Write

1 I've just arrived in  town.

2 I feel at  _____ already.

3 I haven't seen a _____

4 I've  _____ all your old favourites.

5 I've even made you  _____

6 It's time to say _____

6 Write

already   just   yet   yet

Have you seen Ziggy's new video _____ ?

Yes, I've _____ seen it.

Yes, I've _____ seen it.

No, I haven't seen it _____

1 Write

I have to get into the bathroom.

1 She has to get into the bathroom.

I want to go into the bathroom now.

2 _____

_____

I can't find my car keys.

3 _____

_____

I saw your car keys last night.

4 _____

_____

2 Write *for* or *since*

1 Tom's been in the bathroom <u>for</u> five minutes.

2 He's been in the bathroom _____ quarter past seven.

3 I've been at this school _____ 1996.

4 I've had this bicycle _____ two months.

5 Mum and Dad haven't had a holiday _____ three years.

6 They haven't visited Gran _____ June.

❸ Odd one out

1 city   house   town   village   _____

2 football   guitar   tennis   volleyball   _____

3 January   June   October   Wednesday   _____

4 book   cassette   CD   video   _____

5 month   three   week   year   _____

6 Dad   Gran   Mum   Tom   _____

❹ Read and write

She's been at this school for three months.   I've been at this school _____ .

She's been at this school since January.   I've been at this school _____ .

She came to this school three months ago.   I came to this school _____ .

Remember!

❺ Rewrite the sentences

1 I've had my watch for three years.

He's had his watch since _____

He got his watch _____

2 I got my comic four days ago.

She's had her comic for _____

She's had _____

3 I've had my bike since January.

He's had his bike _____

He got _____

4 I've had my computer for two weeks.

She's _____

_____

43

6 **Write questions for your friend**

QUESTIONS

1 When did you first _____ ?

2 How long _____ ?

3 _____ ?

4 _____ ?

7 **Answer your friend's questions**

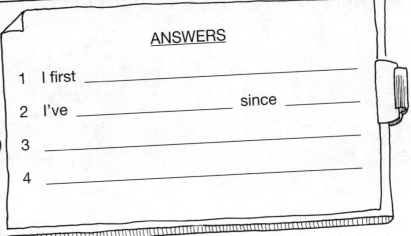

ANSWERS

1 I first _____

2 I've _____ since _____

3 _____

4 _____

8 **Write about your friend**

1 My friend _____

2 _____

3 _____

4 _____

1 **Complete the questions**

1 Planes are made of metal and glass, <u>aren't they?</u>

2 They're not made of paper, _____ ?

3 Planes are very heavy, _____ ?

4 Tom's frightened, _____ ?

5 Susan isn't frightened, _____ ?

6 Tom doesn't want to read Susan's book, _____ ?

2 **Write**   balloon   glass   helicopter   kite   metal   paper   plane   wood

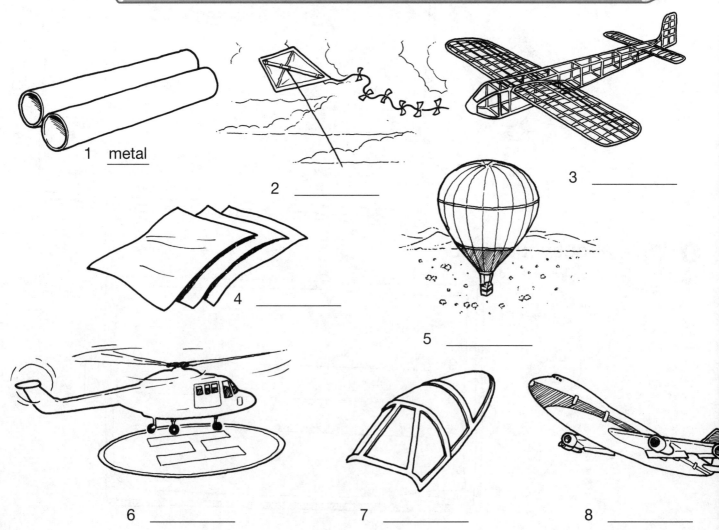

1   <u>metal</u>

2   _____

3   _____

4   _____

5   _____

6   _____

7   _____

8   _____

3 True (✔) or false (✘)?

1 Icarus flew too near the sun. ✓

2 He made wings out of paper.

3 The Wright Brothers' flight was in 1903.

4 Wilbur Wright was the pilot of Flyer I.

5 Igor Sikorsky was born in America.

6 Helicopters can take off vertically.

7 The Montgolfier Brothers filled their balloon with hydrogen.

8 Their balloon flew for less than ten kilometres.

4 Write

built   designed   fell   flew

1 Sikorsky <u>designed</u> the first helicopter.

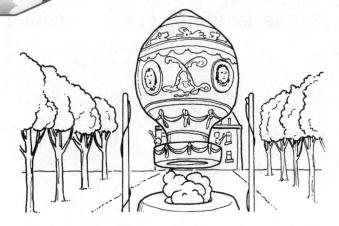

2 The Montgolfiers _____ in a balloon.

3 Icarus _____ into the sea.

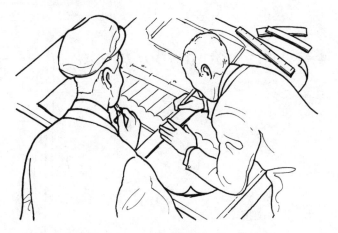

4 The Wright Brothers _____ the first plane with an engine in it.

5 Write questions for your friend

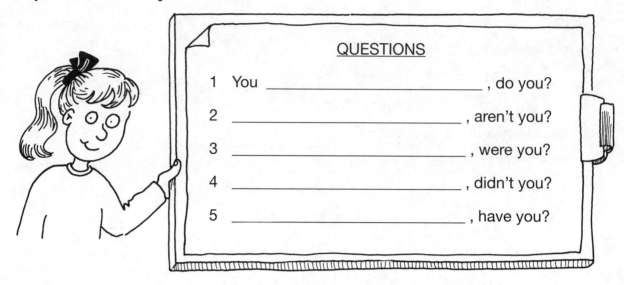

QUESTIONS

1 You _____ , do you?

2 _____ , aren't you?

3 _____ , were you?

4 _____ , didn't you?

5 _____ , have you?

6 Answer your friend's questions

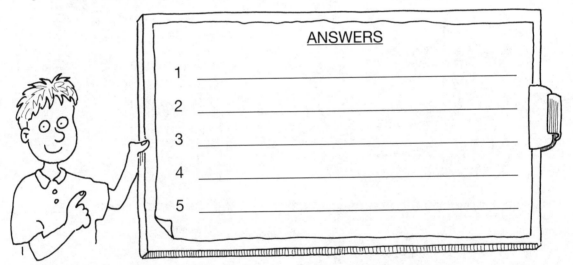

ANSWERS

1 _____

2 _____

3 _____

4 _____

5 _____

7 Write about your friend

1 My friend _____

2 _____

3 _____

4 _____

5 _____

1 Write

ever	
	never
yet	
	already

1 Have you <u>ever</u> met a pop star?

2 I've _____ got all Ziggy's CDs.

3 Why have you _____ been to a concert?

4 Ziggy hasn't arrived here _____

5 Has he _____ sung here before?

2 Write

1 have you heard the news susan tom asked

   'Have you heard the news, Susan?' Tom asked.

2 what's the news tom asked susan

   _____

   _____

3 oh no said susan why didn't you get tickets

   _____

   _____

4 i know said tom we can ask go!man to help us

   _____

   _____

❸ Write *for* or *since*

1   Bruce has worked as a flying doctor <u>for</u> fourteen years.

2   He has had his car _____ three months.

3   He has played the guitar _____ August.

4   He has had his house _____ 1995.

5   He has worn glasses _____ two years.

6   He has had a cold _____ Thursday.

❹ Rewrite the sentences in exercise 3 with *ago*

1   Bruce started working as a flying doctor _____

2   He got his car _____

3   He started _____

4   He got _____

5   He _____

6   _____

❺ Find the words

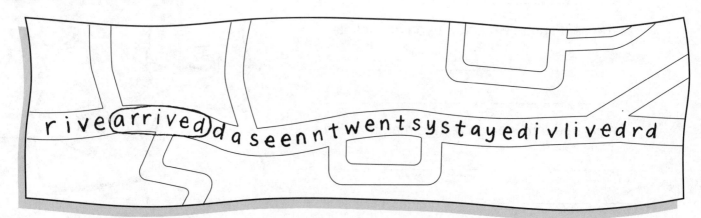

r i v e (a r r i v e d) d a s e e n n t w e n t s y s t a y e d i v l i v e d r d

6 Write replies

1 Planes are made of wood, aren't they?

<u>No, they're made of metal and glass.</u>   [metal and glass]

2 This is an interesting book, isn't it?

_____   [boring]

3 You like flying, don't you?

_____   [hate]

4 The Montgolfier Brothers built a plane, didn't they?

_____   [balloon]

5 Icarus flew too near the moon, didn't he?

_____   [sun]

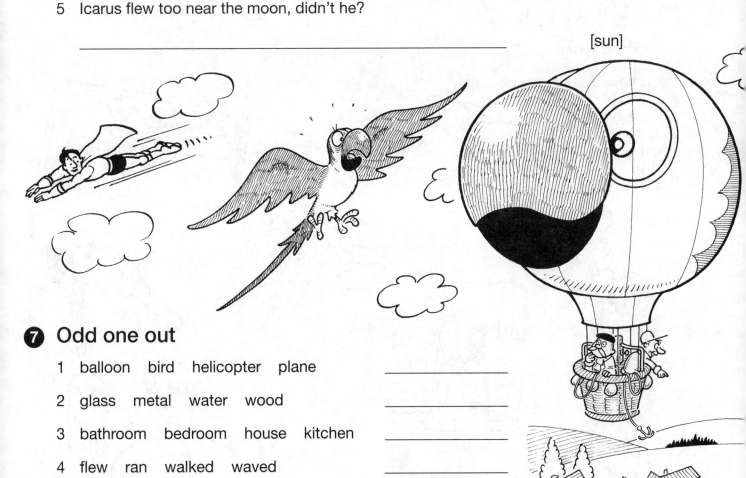

7 Odd one out

1 balloon   bird   helicopter   plane   _____

2 glass   metal   water   wood   _____

3 bathroom   bedroom   house   kitchen   _____

4 flew   ran   walked   waved   _____

5 say   see   shout   sing   _____

6 book   magazine   newspaper   video   _____

⑧ Write

DOWN ↓

1 When does the plane land at the <u>airport</u>?

3 I've just heard Ziggy's latest

_____

4 Let me _____ your bicycle, please.

7 Have you seen Dad's car

_____ ?

ACROSS →

2 Is Ziggy a good <u>singer</u>?

5 I think Tom is _____ of flying.

6 I haven't read a book _____ a year.

8 Let's meet _____ two o'clock.

9 I've only got one _____ for the concert.

10 Susan _____ in the pool every day.

❶ Match and write

1 Tokyo's in Japan.

 Isn't Tokyo its capital?

 Yes, it is.

2 A lot of people live in Tokyo.

 _____

 Yes, it is.

3 Japan is an island country.

 _____

 Yes, it is.

4 Tokyo's on one of the islands.

 _____

 Yes, it is.

Isn't it made up of four islands?

Isn't Tokyo its capital?

Isn't the population nearly twelve million?

Isn't it on the largest island?

❷ Write

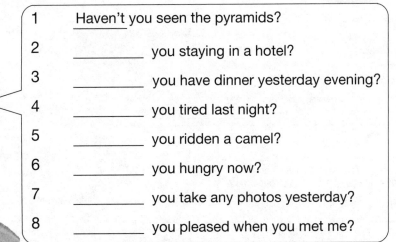

1	Haven't you seen the pyramids?	Yes, I have.
2	_____ you staying in a hotel?	No, I _____
3	_____ you have dinner yesterday evening?	Yes, I _____
4	_____ you tired last night?	No, I _____
5	_____ you ridden a camel?	No, I _____
6	_____ you hungry now?	Yes, I _____
7	_____ you take any photos yesterday?	No, I _____
8	_____ you pleased when you met me?	Yes, I _____

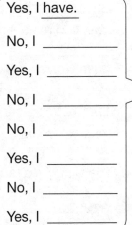

❸ Write

1. I think the Amazon is the longest river in the world.

   Isn't the Nile the longest river in the world?

   Yes, you're right.

2. The Nile flows from Lake Rudolf, doesn't it?

   Doesn't _____ ?

   Yes, you're right.

3. The Nile is 7,670 kilometres long.

   _____ ?

   Yes, you're right.

4. People haven't lived on the banks of the Nile for very long.

   _____ ?

   Yes, you're right.

5. The Aswan Dam's on the borders of Egypt and Libya, isn't it?

   _____ ?

   Yes, you're right.

6. I think President Nasser opened the dam in 1970.

   _____ ?

   Yes, you're right.

7. Lake Nasser is quite small.

   _____ ?

   Yes, you're right.

8. The Nile gives farmers water in the winter only.

   _____ ?

   Yes, you're right.

Cairo

EGYPT

Luxor

Aswan
Dam

SUDAN

UGANDA

Lake
Victoria

4 Write questions for your friend

QUESTIONS

1 Haven't _____ ?

2 Aren't _____ ?

3 Didn't _____ ?

4 Weren't _____ ?

5 _____ ?

6 _____ ?

5 Answer your friend's questions

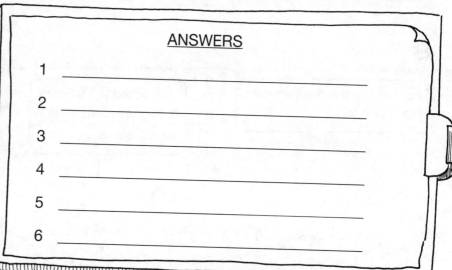

ANSWERS

1 _____

2 _____

3 _____

4 _____

5 _____

6 _____

6 Write about your friend

1 My friend _____

2 _____

3 _____

4 _____

5 _____

6 _____

1 Write

her herself him himself me myself ourselves
them themselves us you you yourself yourselves

I	you	he	she
me	you	_____	_____
myself	_____	_____	_____

we	you	they
_____	_____	_____
_____	_____	_____

2 Write

1 I didn't cut the grass myself. You cut it for me.

2 We picked the flowers ourselves. They didn't pick them for us.

3 I washed the car for you. You _____ _____ _____

4 We didn't feed the cat for you. You _____ _____

5 She dug the garden herself. He _____ _____

6 We tidied the living room for them. They _____ _____

3 **Write**

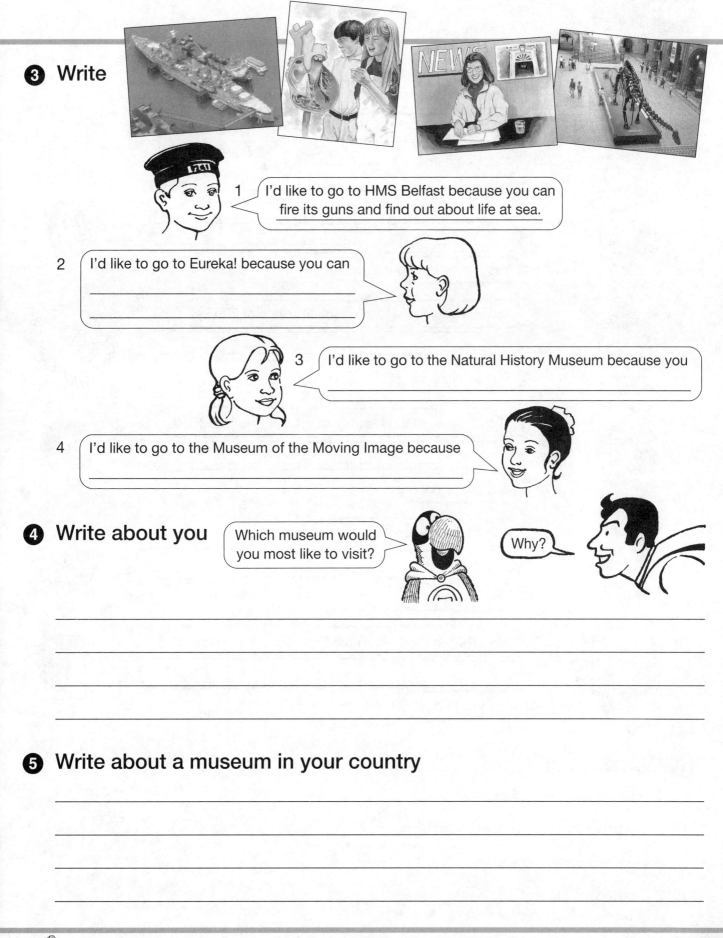

1 I'd like to go to HMS Belfast because you can fire its guns and find out about life at sea.

2 I'd like to go to Eureka! because you can
_____
_____

3 I'd like to go to the Natural History Museum because you
_____

4 I'd like to go to the Museum of the Moving Image because
_____

4 **Write about you**

Which museum would you most like to visit?

Why?

_____
_____
_____
_____

5 **Write about a museum in your country**

_____
_____
_____
_____

6 **Write**

1 I think The Natural History Museum opened in 1906.

Didn't it open in 1896?

Yes, you're right.

2 The model dinosaurs there are made of paper.

_____ ?

Yes, you're right.

3 You can only listen to and look at things at Eureka!

_____ ?

Yes, you're right.

4 The Museum of the Moving Image is known as MUMI.

_____ ?

Yes, you're right.

5 I think HMS Belfast is a plane.

_____ ?

Yes, you're right.

6 HMS Belfast took part in the First World War, didn't it?

_____ ?

Yes, you're right.

7 **Odd one out**

1 car   museum   plane   ship   _____

2 marble   metal   model   plastic   _____

3 bones   look   smell   touch   _____

4 cartoons   films   the news   video   _____

1 Write

a | 1100 – 1199   <u>twelfth century</u>

d | _____ nineteenth century

b | _____ fifteenth century

e | 1900 – 1999 _____

c | 1600 – 1699 _____

f | _____ twenty-first century

2 Write

designer   emperor   engineer   explorer   pilot   queen

17th century   18th century   19th century   19th century
20th century   20th century

1 Captain Cook <u>was an</u>
   <u>explorer who lived in the</u>
   <u>18th century.</u>

4 Amy Johnson _____
   _____
   _____

2 Gustave Eiffel _____
   _____
   _____

3 Shah Jahan _____
   _____
   _____

5 Igor Sikorsky _____
   _____
   _____

6 Victoria _____
   _____
   _____

❸ Match and write

Elizabeth I was a queen who

died in 1603

_____

_____

Victoria was a queen who

_____

_____

ruled Great Britain for 64 years
died in 1603
was born in 1819
became queen in 1558
lived in the 19th century
never married

DIEU ET MON DROIT

❹ Write

1 Elizabeth I was a queen who ruled <u>for 45 years.</u>

2 Victoria was a queen who died _____

3 Elizabeth I was a queen who was _____

4 Victoria was a woman who became _____

5 Elizabeth I was a queen who lived _____

5 **Match**

1   Captain Cook sailed in a ship which   was very small.

2   Gustave Eiffel built a tower which   left England in 1768.

3   Shah Jahan built a palace which   were about the lives of poor people.

4   Amy Johnson flew in a plane which   was the highest in the world until 1930.

5   Igor Sikorsky designed a helicopter which   was made of marble.

6   Charles Dickens wrote books which   could fly backwards.

6 **Write your own sentences**

1   The Taj Mahal is a palace which _____

2   Flyer I was a plane which _____

3   Neil Armstrong was an astronaut who _____

4   The Great Wall of China is a wall which _____

5   HMS Belfast was a ship which _____

6   Sir Walter Raleigh was an explorer who _____

UNIT **20**

1 Write

bury call discover fill find make open see steal touch

found made buried filled opened stolen
called saw discovered touched

bury _____ _____ _____ _____

buried _____ _____ _____ _____

make _____ _____ _____ _____

_____ _____ _____ _____

2 Write

1 Tutankhamun was <u>buried</u> on the west bank of the Nile.

2 His tomb was _____ with jewels and other wonderful things.

3 His tomb was never _____ by thieves.

4 Its treasures weren't _____

5 Tutankhamun's tomb was _____ by a British archaeologist.

6 The archaeologist was _____ Howard Carter.

7 Nothing in the tomb was _____

8 When the tomb was _____ , Carter saw many wonderful things.

3 Write

Khufu's pyramid is

1 at <u>Gizeh</u>

2 137 _____

3 the _____

4 called _____

4 Match and write

> which are a symbol of Egypt
> which is near Cairo
> who worked for twenty years
> which are triangles
> who was an ancient Egyptian king
> which were very heavy

1 The Great Pyramid is at Gizeh, <u>which is near Cairo</u>.

2 Khufu, _____ , was buried in the Great Pyramid.

3 100,000 men, _____ , built the Great Pyramid.

4 The sides of pyramids, _____ , meet at the top.

5 Two million blocks of stone, _____ , were used
   to build the Great Pyramid.

6 The pyramids, _____ , are on postage stamps.

5 Write

1 I think pyramids have got three sides.

Haven't they got four sides?

Yes, you're right.

2 I think Tutankhamun's tomb was discovered in 1921.

_____ ?

Yes, you're right.

3 I think an American archaeologist discovered it.

_____ ?

Yes, you're right.

4 I think the Great Pyramid is at Saqqara.

_____ ?

Yes, you're right.

6 Complete the sentences

1 Tom wrote the letter himself. Mum didn't write it for him.

2 We didn't clean our bikes _____ . My dad cleaned _____ for _____

3 Susan washed her hair _____ . Mum didn't wash _____ for _____

4 I didn't clean my shoes _____ . My dad cleaned _____ for _____

5 Tom and Susan made dinner _____ . Mum didn't make _____ for _____

7 Write *who* or *which*

1 Sherif is a boy <u>who</u> lives in Cairo.

2 The Nile, _____ is 6,670 kilometres long, is the longest river in the world.

3 HMS Belfast is a ship _____ is a museum.

4 Napoleon was an emperor _____ visited Egypt.

5 William Shakespeare, _____ wrote many plays, is the most famous Elizabethan writer.

6 I like books _____ are about dinosaurs.

7 Tutankhamun was a king _____ died when he was very young.

8 The biggest pyramid in Mexico is at Cholula, _____ is near Mexico City.

8 Write

The Ancient Egyptians	**In Ancient Egypt**
1 called their kings Pharaohs.	the kings <u>were called Pharaohs.</u>
2 built pyramids for their kings.	pyramids _____
3 buried their kings in tombs.	the kings _____
4 filled the tombs with beautiful things.	the tombs _____ _____
5 put tables and chairs in the tombs.	chairs and tables _____ _____
6 grew crops near the Nile.	crops _____

1 **Match and write**

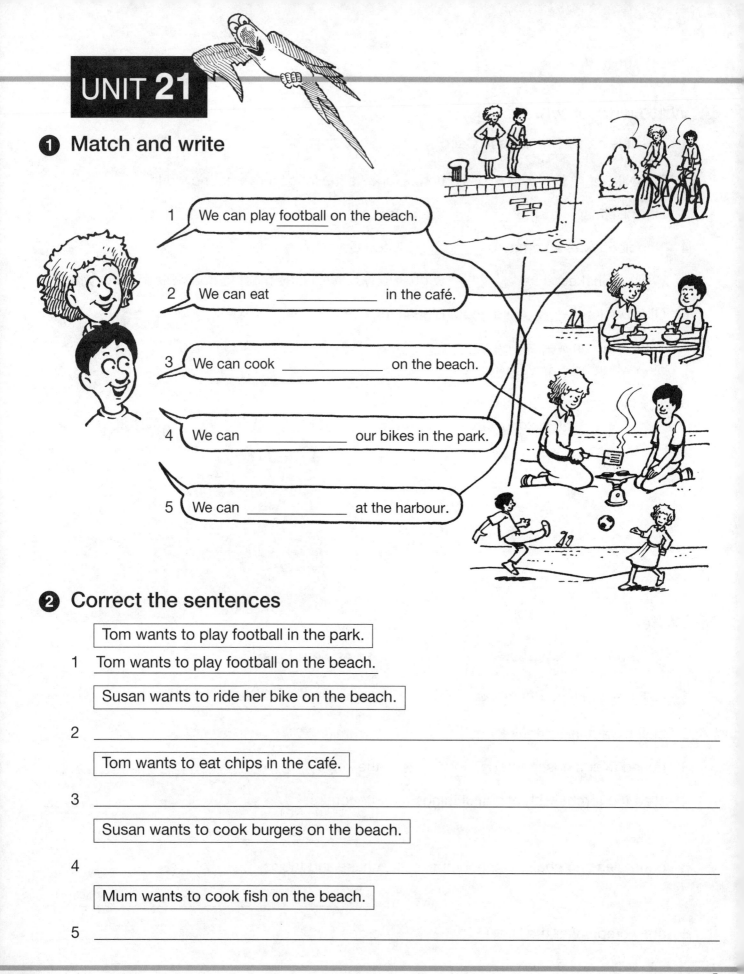

1 We can play football on the beach.

2 We can eat _____ in the café.

3 We can cook _____ on the beach.

4 We can _____ our bikes in the park.

5 We can _____ at the harbour.

2 **Correct the sentences**

Tom wants to play football in the park.

1 Tom wants to play football on the beach.

Susan wants to ride her bike on the beach.

2 _____

Tom wants to eat chips in the café.

3 _____

Susan wants to cook burgers on the beach.

4 _____

Mum wants to cook fish on the beach.

5 _____

3 Odd one out

1 cycling eating fishing football _____

2 fish harbour burgers ice cream _____

3 cold freezing hot small _____

4 beach bike café park _____

4 Write

1 They didn't go on a boat.

2 Dad _____ cola.

3 Susan _____ a T-shirt.

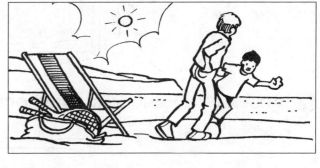

4 They _____ tennis.

5 Mum _____ swimming.

6 They _____ fish and chips.

5 Write in or *on*

1 I'd love to swim <u>in</u> the sea.

2 Dad likes to sleep _____ the beach.

3 Can we play football _____ the park?

4 You can have a ride _____ my bike.

5 It's too hot _____ the car.

6 Write questions for your friend

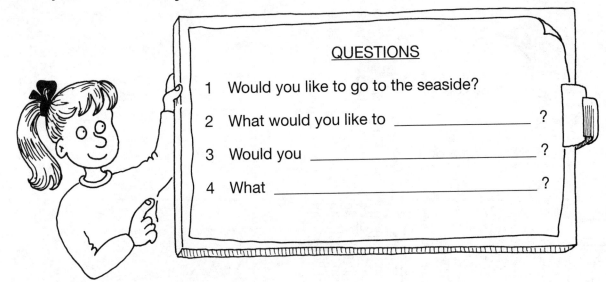

QUESTIONS

1 Would you like to go to the seaside?

2 What would you like to _____ ?

3 Would you _____ ?

4 What _____ ?

7 Answer your friend's questions

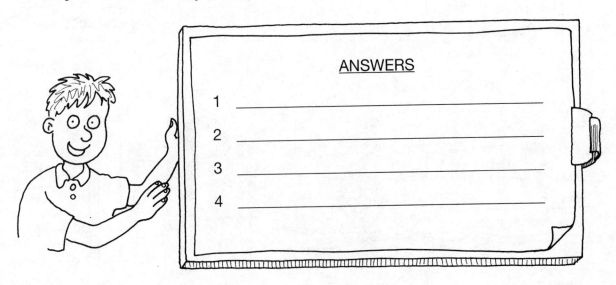

ANSWERS

1 _____

2 _____

3 _____

4 _____

1 Write

cod   diving   fishing   gold   Italian   port   Spanish   treasure

Judy Hill

treasure

_____

_____

_____

Martin Lopez

cod

_____

_____

_____

2 True (✔) or false (✗)?

1   Judy is a diver.   ✔

2   The *Liberta* is a Spanish ship.

3   It lies on the sea bed.

4   Martin lives in Spain.

5   He goes fishing once a week.

6   There are lots of cod near Vigo.

3 Find the words and write

a	r	t	n	o	u	v	e	d	a
p	o	t	s	s	f	i	p	i	r
w	n	e	o	e	i	t	o	v	t
o	t	r	e	a	s	u	r	e	p
g	o	l	d	j	h	k	t	r	l
h	f	g	e	a	c	c	v	b	n
m	x	q	u	j	d	s	r	a	o
r	s	e	c	a	s	h	i	p	a

1   fish

2 _____

3 _____

4 _____

5 _____

6 _____

7 _____

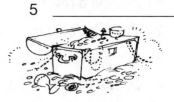

8 _____

4 Write

I've been a diver for five years.

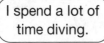

I spend a lot of time diving.

I found an old silver cup.

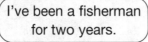

I've been a fisherman for two years.

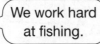

We work hard at fishing.

I work with my son.

1   She's been a diver for five years.

2 _____

3 _____

4 _____

5 _____

6 _____

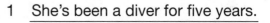

⑤ Match and write

1 The old fisherman <u>was</u> very poor.

2 The other fishermen _____ at him.

3 One day he _____ a very big fish.

4 He _____ a big piece of fish on his hook.

5 The fish _____ the boat for hours.

6 The fishing line _____

⑥ Find the words

fi line tchookerbtboatinsharbourmaisailrerportiote

1 Read and write

1 She drives over the Golden Gate bridge every day. [c]

2 She appeared in a film last year. [ ]

3 She goes to the beach every week. [ ]

4 She wears a big coat in winter. [ ]

2 Match and write

Rio de Janeiro	Russian	Pacific
Mumbai	Brazilian	Baltic
San Francisco	Indian	Indian
St Petersburg	American	Atlantic

1 Rio de Janeiro is a Brazilian city which is on the Atlantic Ocean.

2 _____

3 _____

4 _____

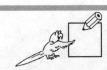

❸ Odd one out

1 Canberra   Mexico City   Russia   San Francisco   _____

2 Atlantic   Baltic   Pacific   Thames   _____

3 Istanbul   London   Paris   Washington   _____

4 France   Mumbai   Turkey   USA   _____

❹ Write

1 I think San Francisco is the capital of the USA.

Isn't Washington the capital of the USA?

Yes, you're right.

2 I think Paris is in Italy.

Isn't _____ France?

_____

3 I think Lincoln was the first president of the USA.

Wasn't Washington _____ ?

_____

4 I think Mumbai is on the Pacific Ocean.

_____ ?

_____

5 I think St Petersburg is the capital of Russia.

_____ ?

_____

6 I think Alexandria is on the River Nile.

_____ ?

_____

5 **Write**

1 California is the <u>biggest state</u> in the USA.

2 Los Angeles is in the _____ of California.

3 San Francisco was _____ on steep hills.

4 _____ love to ride on the cable cars in San Francisco.

5 They love to eat _____ at Fisherman's Wharf.

6 There are many Mexican, _____ and Chinese people in San Francisco.

6 **Write the words in order**

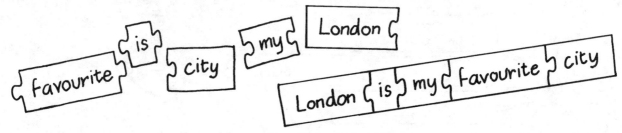

1 favourite is city my London

   <u>London is my favourite city.</u>

2 visited year London I last friend with my

   _____

3 took on trip we the Thames River boat a

   _____

4 bridges lot a of sailed we under

   _____

UNIT 24

1 **Match and write**

1 Susan <u>is playing</u> tennis in the <u>park.</u>

2 Dad _____ a

   newspaper on the _____

3 Mum _____ a hat in

   the _____

4 Tom _____ an ice

   cream in the _____

2 **Write**

fell   had   played   rode   shone   started   swam   went

Dear Mum,

We <u>had</u> a wonderful day at Portsea yesterday. The sun _____

and it wasn't cold. Tom _____ in the sea – he was blue with

cold! We _____ football on the beach. After that John sat in a

deckchair and _____ asleep! Then the children _____

their bikes in the park. John and I went for a walk. Then it _____

raining and we _____ home.

Hope you are well.

   Love,

      Jane

3 Write *who* or *which*

1 Judy is a diver <u>who</u> looks for treasure.

2 She has found a ship _____ was wrecked a long time ago.

3 The ship, _____ is on the sea bed, is Italian.

4 The cup, _____ Judy found, was made in Venice.

5 Martin is a fisherman _____ lives in Vigo.

6 Vigo, _____ is a port, is in Spain.

7 Andres is someone _____ sails with Martin and his son.

8 Paco, _____ wants to go to university, has been a fisherman for two years.

4 Write

1 you are too old to fish old man they said

'You are too old to fish, old man,' they said.

2 you are tired fish the old man said i will kill you now

_____

3 did you catch a big fish today old man they laughed

_____

4 where is your fish they asked we do not see it

_____

5 i caught a big fish the old man replied but the sharks ate it

_____

75

5 **Find the words**

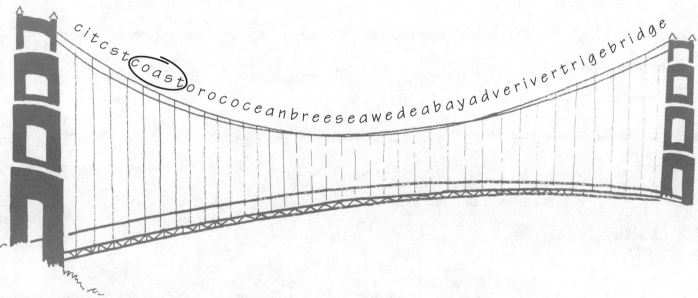

citcst coast *orococeanbreeseawedeabayadverivertrigebridge*

6 **Write**

1 Sita is going to <u>appear</u> in a film.

2 People in Rio love to _____ !

3 They often go to the _____ too.

4 Alcatraz is an _____ in San Francisco Bay.

5 Many people who live in San Francisco were born

in _____

6 _____ lives in St Petersburg.

a	p	p	e	a	r
	a				
		a			
			a		
				a	
					a

7 **Write your own words and sentences**

1 _____

2 _____

3 _____

4 _____

5 _____

6 _____

a					
	a				
		a			
			a		
				a	
					a

8 Write

Last week strong <u>winds</u> drove an oil _____ onto rocks off the Scottish _____ .

The _____ , which was Swedish, ran aground on February the nineteenth. It was

carrying 80,000 tons of _____ . When the _____ ran aground, _____

started leaking into the _____ . The strong _____ continued and the _____

began to break up. Then the _____ began to pour into the _____ , where it killed

many _____ . It then spread to the _____ , which are now black. A clean-up

_____ has started but it will take time and _____ to remove the _____

from the _____ .

9 Write

1 The coast <u>was lashed</u> by strong winds.   [lash]

2 The tanker _____ onto rocks.   [drive]

3 It _____ in two by the sea.   [break]

4 Thousands of birds _____ by the oil.   [kill]

5 Dead birds _____ on the coast.   [wash up]

6 Some of the oil _____ from the beaches.   [remove]

CONDITIONALS

If I look up, I can see the sky. If you look up, you can see the sky. If he looks up, he can see the sky. If she looks up, she can see the sky. If we look up, we can see the sky. If you look up, you can see the sky. If they look up, they can see the sky.

If I eat too much, I'll get fat. If you eat too much, you'll get fat. If he eats too much, he'll get fat. If she eats too much, she'll get fat. If we eat too much, we'll get fat. If you eat too much, you'll get fat. If they eat too much, they'll get fat.

- We use these conditionals when it is possible that the situation expressed in the *if*-clause will happen in the future. For example, it is very possible that I will eat too much, and so I will get fat.
- Although this can only happen in the future, we use the present simple tense in the *if*-clause.
- The order of the clauses can be reversed:
  You can see the sky if you look up.
- Note that when *if* is in the middle of the sentence, there is no need for a comma (,) to divide the two clauses.

PASSIVE

present simple passive

Tea is grown in China. Oil and coal are produced in America.

past simple passive

Last week a tanker was driven onto rocks. The Pharaohs were buried in tombs.

- We use the passive when a) we do not know who carried out the action or b) it doesn't matter who carried out the action. The use of the passive focuses attention on the thing or person who has had the action done to them (a tanker, the Pharaohs).
- If we are interested in who carried out the action, we can use *by* with the passive:
  Tutankhamun's tomb was discovered by Howard Carter.

COMPARISON OF ADVERBS

fast   faster   fastest

carefully   more carefully   the most carefully

Ben can swim fast. Ben can swim faster than anyone in the class. Ben can swim the fastest in his class.

Susan can write carefully. Susan can write more carefully than her brother. Susan can write the most carefully in her family.

- Often we prefer to use comparative and superlative adjectives with nouns to express the above meanings:
  Ben is the fastest swimmer in his class.   *Susan is the most careful writer in her family.*

- Note the following irregular forms:
  well   better   best   *badly   worse   worst*

RELATIVE CLAUSES

> who   which   that

1   Defining

> The man who wrote *Oliver Twist* was Charles Dickens.
> Dickens wrote books which described the life of poor people.
> The book that I like best is *David Copperfield*.

- Defining relative clauses tell you which man or book(s) you mean. These clauses are an essential part of the meaning of the sentence.

2   Non-defining

> Sita, who lives in Mumbai, is a film star.
> San Francisco, which is on the Pacific, is a beautiful city.

- Non-defining clauses give additional information about the subject of the sentence. They do not form an essential part of the meaning of the sentence.
- They are separated from the rest of the sentence by commas.

QUESTION TAGS

> Planes are amazing, aren't they?   Yes, they are.
> She loves him, doesn't she?   Yes, she does.

> They aren't heavy, are they?   No, they aren't.
> You don't like flying, do you?   No, I don't.

- We use question tags when we expect the person we are speaking to to agree with the statement. We are sure that the statement is correct. We expect the answers given above.

NEGATIVE QUESTIONS

> Isn't Cairo the capital of Egypt?   Yes, it is.
> Don't you like London?   No, I don't.

- Here the first speaker is not sure of the answer to the question. The second speaker can either agree or disagree with the statement questioned.
- Sometimes we use this negative question form to express doubt about a statement. It is a polite way of saying that you think the speaker is wrong:
  Speaker 1 *The Amazon is the longest river in the world.*
  Speaker 2 *Isn't the Nile the longest river in the world?*
  Speaker 1 *Yes, I think you're right.*

Your Child at L

Look out for me on the pages of this book.

Working at home with your child can be a very enjoyable shared experience. It is also an invaluable part of his or her education.

This book gives a selection of activities most 4-year-olds will be able to perform and enjoy. It is designed for pre-school children working towards school entry.

All the activities in this book practise important skills in the three core subjects, Mathematics, English and Science. The Notes for Parents overleaf include simple symbols to show which subject skills are practised in each activity.

 Maths   English   Science

You can help your child to get the best out of this book by:

 finding a quiet time when you are both relaxed and undisturbed. Enjoy the time together and the activity.

 letting your child help select an activity.

talking about each activity, exchanging opinions and working out problems. This develops your child's speaking and listening skills, which will help all other areas of learning.

 writing down answers to questions on some activities.

 trying to finish on a positive point, before your child gets tired. Let him or her control the pace.

 always giving plenty of praise and encouragement. Everyone responds well if they feel they are succeeding.

Rhona Whiteford and Jim Fitzsimmons
Illustrated by Sasha Lipscomb

BROCKHAMPTON PRESS
LONDON

NOTES FOR PARENTS

Page 4 Yummy cakes M E

Introduces the idea of sorting and classifying everyday objects according to shape and colour. Encourage your child to look for similarities in familiar things, so that they can begin to see relationships.

Page 5 Fill it up M E

This is an exercise in comparing size and capacity. There is no substitute for practical experience, so try out the task.

Pages 6-7 Counting to 5 M E

This is designed to help your child link a quantity with a numeral. To reinforce this, count out real objects and write the numeral on a piece of paper.

Pages 8-9 3 Little dogs M E S

An exercise in practical counting as well as construction. Your child has to make the quantity required to fulfil a real purpose. You can help further by asking questions such as, 'Is there a bed for each dog?', or 'Has each dog got a biscuit?'.

Page 10 Shapes all around M E

Use the pictures to help your child recognise simple 3D shapes. After you have looked at the pictures help him or her to 'find' some of the shapes around the house.

Page 11 Building time M E

This activity helps your child to discover some of the properties of 3D shapes through simple building tasks.

Page 12 Time to count M E

This activity gives your child the opportunity to write numerals 1,2,3 and link them with the quantity.

Page 13 Things I like to do E

This is a good topic for discussion with any young child. Do offer your opinions to encourage your child to develop listening as well as speaking skills.

Pages 14-15 Starting to write E

These are easy exercises to develop hand control and the left-to-right movement needed for reading and writing. They will also encourage your child to look for similarities and differences, which helps prepare for reading and writing.

Page 16 My favourite books E

This exercise asks your child to put preferences in order.

Page 17 A drawing page E

This is designed to help the development of a basic drawing vocabulary, hand control, and a sense of achievement in completing a picture.

Page 18 Look carefully

A simple set of puzzles to develop visual discrimination, and scanning and matching skills, which help prepare your child for reading and writing.

Page 19 Listen carefully

This game helps to develop the vital skill of listening. It also encourages social awareness and co-operation.

Page 20 Umbrella fun

Ask your child to complete the patterns on the umbrella in the same colours. This exercise is important for pre-reading and writing development in that the child must scan the whole page, match symbols, complete patterns and look for details.

Page 21 Things I can do S

This exercise is to help your child make a record of personal skills. If you keep this record and refer to it after a period of time it will help your child to see that skills can be developed over time.

Pages 22-23 Living and non-living S E

This is a discussion and observation activity. You will need to help your child to develop the concept of what constitutes a 'living' thing and what constitutes a 'non-living' thing.

Page 24 Looking at materials S E

This discussion and observation exercise explores the variety of materials available today. Help enlarge your child's vocabulary by suggesting descriptive words.

Page 25 Weather S E

This discussion and observation task draws on your child's own experience. Encourage your child to think about this activity by talking about ways to keep cool or warm.

Page 26 Shadows S E

Observation of light and shadow in a play situation will help focus your child's attention and promote discussion and further learning.

Page 27 Moving toys S E

This is a chance to experiment with different sources of movement energy and look at how it is stored. Ask questions to encourage your child to discover the power source of things.

Pages 28-29 Build a tower S E

Practical experience of making stable structures from different materials and on different surfaces. Ask your child what he or she notices about the different surfaces.

Page 30 In the kitchen S E

This task encourages recognition of the senses and asks your child to make personal choices. Make sure that your child is aware that some substances should never be tasted.

Page 31 My garden S E

Practical experience of planning and creating a pleasing environment and observing living things. Encourage your child to take care of the garden as an on-going task to learn about what living things need to sustain life.

Yummy cakes

Look at the shapes and sizes of these cakes.

I like eclairs best.

My favourites are the jam tarts.

Draw a circle round the cakes which are the same.

Fill it up

Find a spare sock.

Now see how many things you can fit into it.
Look all round the house for things to try.

Find an empty matchbox and see how many things you can fit into it and still be able to open and close it easily.

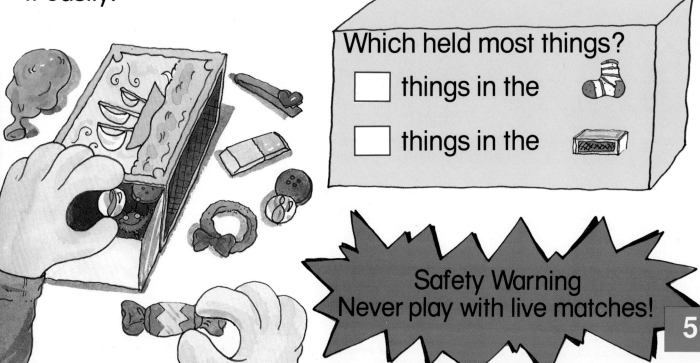

Which held most things?

☐ things in the 🧦

☐ things in the 📦

Safety Warning
Never play with live matches!

5

Counting to 5

Can you count all these things and write the number in the box?

☐ astronauts

☐ craters on the moon

☐ alien

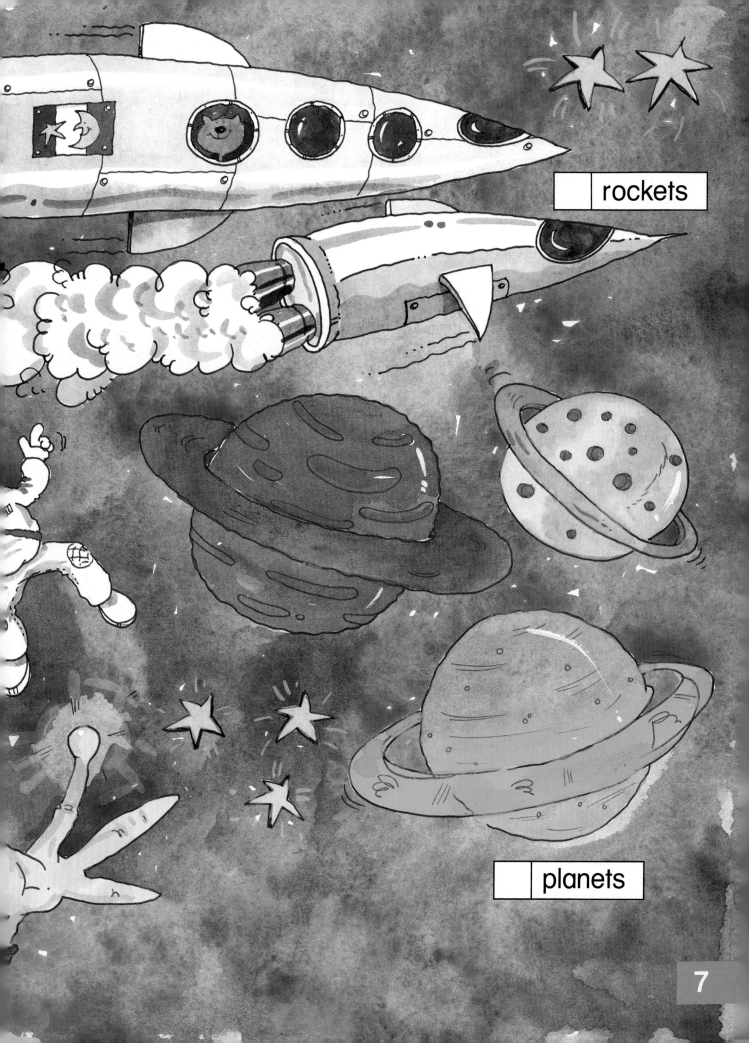

rockets

planets

7

3 little dogs

We need a bed for each little dog. Make them from playdoh.

1 Make a ball.

2 Flatten it.

3 Bend up the sides.

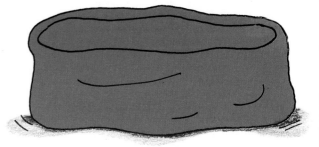

I made ☐ beds.

Ask a grown-up to trace the dogs and cut them out.

Now put each dog in its bed.

8

Now make a playdoh biscuit for each dog and put the biscuits in these bowls.

I made ☐ biscuits.

Sally

Rover

Spotty

Shapes all around

What shapes can you find in this picture?

Tick the shapes you find.

cone ☐

sphere ☐

cylinder ☐

cuboid ☐

cube ☐

Building time!

Find things round your house to use here.

Can you build these structures out of the different shapes? Tick ✓ for 'yes' or cross ✗ for 'no'.

cylinders ☐

cuboids ☐

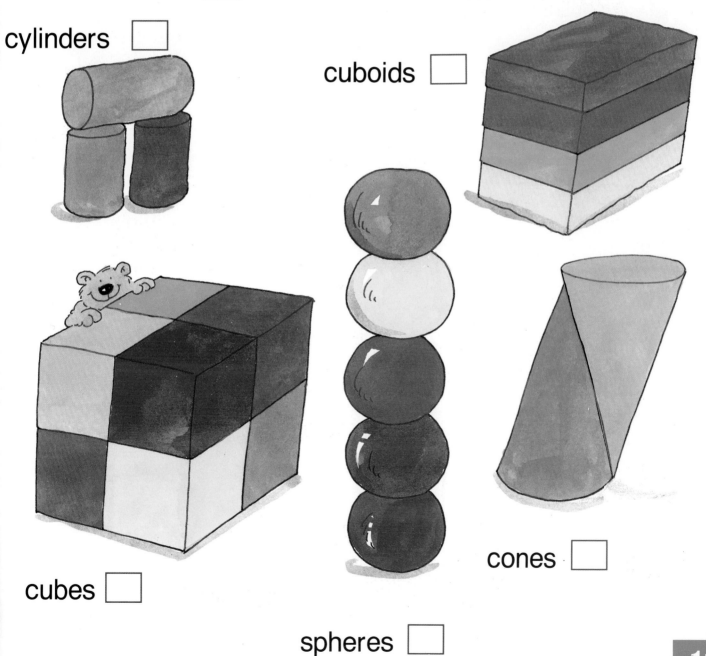

cubes ☐

spheres ☐

cones ☐

Time to count

Draw 1 delicious cake on the plate.

Give me 2 balloons please.

Draw 3 flowers in my flowerpot.

12

Things I like to do

Draw the thing you like doing most.

listening to music 	dancing 	football 	watching TV 
listening to a story 			playing 
eating 			going to the park 
swimming 	helping Mum and Dad 	painting 	drawing 

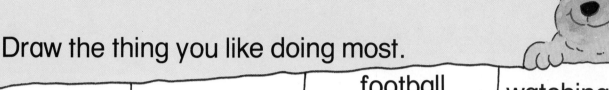

Starting to write

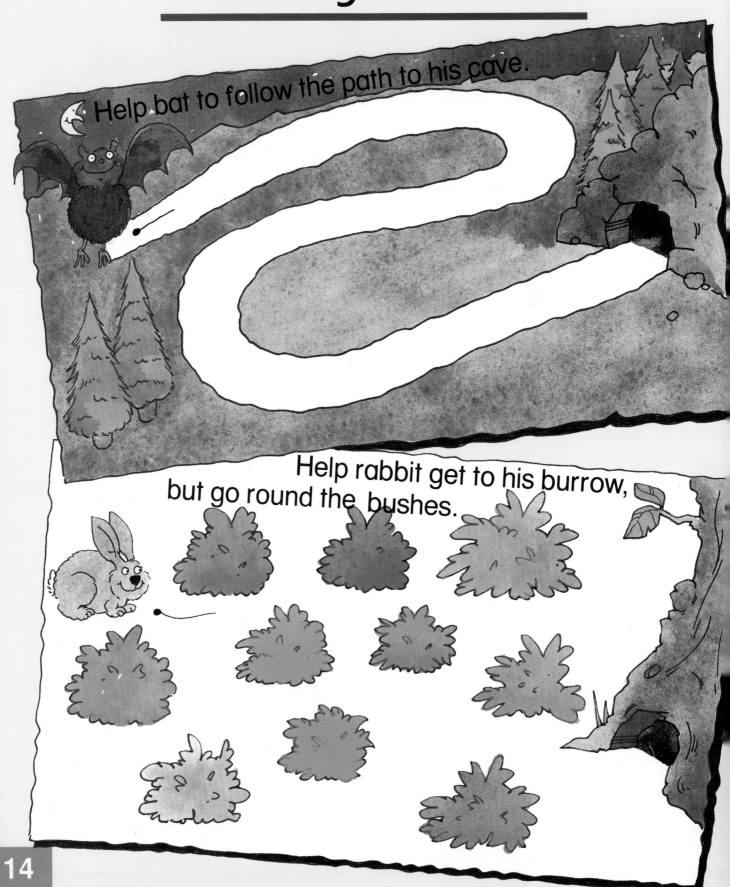

Help bat to follow the path to his cave.

Help rabbit get to his burrow, but go round the bushes.

14

Join the dots to complete the picture.

Look at Jolly Owl. Can you make Olly Owl look just like him?

Jolly

Olly

My favourite books

Ask a grown-up to write your 3 favourite books here.

1st ————————————

2nd ————————————

3rd ————————————

Draw your favourite book character here.

A drawing page

Finish these pictures using the same colours.

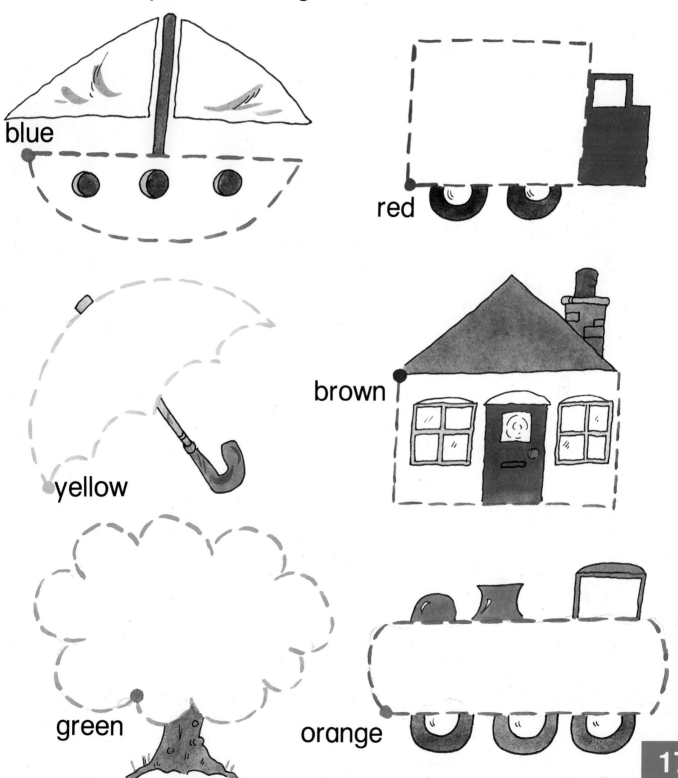

blue

red

yellow

brown

green

orange

Look carefully

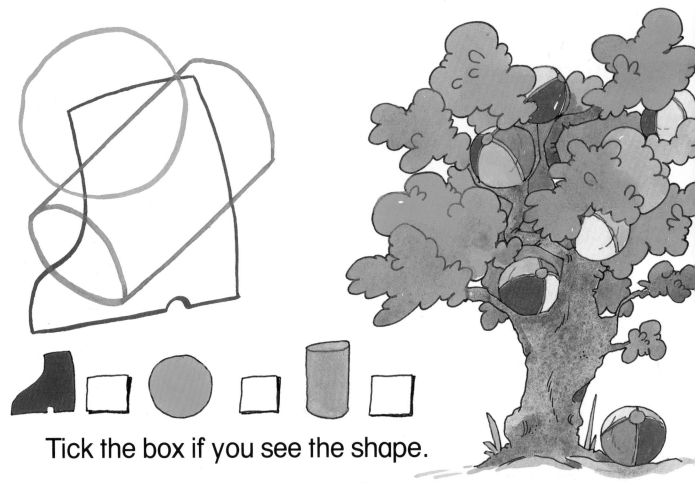

Tick the box if you see the shape.

Can you spot 6 balls here?

Circle the shape which matches the first one.

Listen carefully

Find 6 things round your house which make a noise.

Have you heard these noises?

Now play a listening game. Take turns.

Umbrella fun

Can you finish the patterns on this umbrella?

Things I can do

Try these things and put a tick in the box if you can do them.

run ☐

jump ☐

hop ☐

p with
be ☐

forward roll ☐

ride a bike ☐

row a ball ☐

catch a ball ☐

bat a ball ☐

Do you know which parts of your body you used to do each thing?

21

Living and non-living

Look at these pictures.
Do you know which are pictures of living things and which are of non-living things? Talk about each thing with a grown-up.

Colour the circles red for non-living things and green for living things.

snail

plant

hairdryer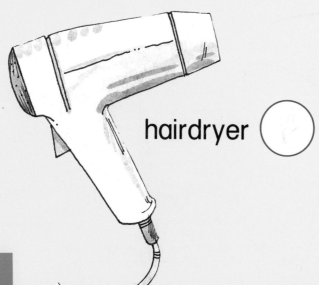

tree

television ○

pair of shoes ○

bike ○

rabbit ○

fish ○

plate of food ○

23

Looking at materials

Look around the house and find as many different bits of materials as you can.

Stick flat ones on this page in the right places.

MY COLLECTION

This is rough.

This is smooth.

This is hard.

This is soft.

This is bumpy.

This is slippery.

This is spongy.

This is sticky.

This is squashy.

Weather

Complete these pictures by drawing the kind of weather you think goes with the clothes shown.

sunshine   rain   snow

Shadows

Go outside on a sunny day
and look for your shadow!

Can you…

Make a tiny
shadow?

Make a long
shadow?

Pat a shadow
on the head?

Pat a friend's
shadow with your
shadow's hand?

Make a wide
shadow?

Make a
jumping
shadow?

Do you know what makes
a shadow appear?

Make a shadow creature

Moving toys

See how many moving toys you have.

Make a collection like this.

What makes them move?

pushing

battery

clockwork

wind up elastic

pulling

the wind

rolling

spring

Build a tower

Can you make a tower that stands up on its own?

Try making a tower from any of these building bricks.

Duplo or Lego

Stickle bricks

wooden bricks or dominoes

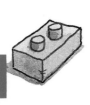

What do you notice if you build on these different surfaces?

1 table

2 fluffy rug

3 sponge

4 towel

How many bricks high was your tallest tower?

My tallest tower was ☐ bricks high.

It was made with_____.

It was built on_____.

In the kitchen

Use all of your senses to test these foodstuffs.

taste

smell

touch

listen

look

Foodstuff	like ✓	dislike ✗
salt		
sugar		
jam		
ketchup		
vinegar		
coffee		
tea		
pepper		
cereal		

Ask an adult to help you taste, touch, smell and look at these foodstuffs. If it is in a container give it a shake. Does it make any sound?

Decide which of these things you like and fill in the chart above.

My little garden

Make your very own garden.

Use an old tin tray or bowl as your container.

Fill the tray with soil or compost.

Use lolly sticks or twigs for trees.

A silver pie dish makes a great pond.

Use an old spoon to dig.

Make a garden path with small pebbles.

Plant these things in your garden:

- carrot tops
- cress seeds
- apple pips
- orange pips
- small weeds from the garden - pull up carefully
- other seeds from fruit you've eaten

Water the plants after you plant them, then water a little every day.

A complete home-learning range.

Have fun with Headstart!

British Library Cataloguing in Publication Data
Whiteford, Rhona
 Your Child at 4
 I. Title II. Fitzsimmons, Jim
 649

ISBN 1-86019-505-9

First Published 1993

© 1993 Rhona Whiteford and Jim Fitzsimmons

This edition published 1997 by Brockhampton Press, a member of
Hodder Headline PLC Group.
10 9 8 7 6 5 4 3
1999 1998 1997

Printed in India.

Photography: Roddy Paine, Tunbridge Wells.